Little
Pebble™

Colorful Foods

Red Foods

by Martha E. H. Rustad

CAPSTONE PRESS
a capstone imprint

Little Pebble is published by Capstone Press,
1710 Roe Crest Drive, North Mankato, Minnesota 56003
www.mycapstone.com

Library of Congress Cataloging-in-Publication Data
Names: Rustad, Martha E. H. (Martha Elizabeth Hillman), 1975– author.
Title: Red foods / by Martha E. H. Rustad.
Description: North Mankato, Minnesota : Capstone Press, [2017] | Audience:
Ages 4–7. | Audience: K to grade 3. | Includes bibliographical references and index.
Identifiers: LCCN 2016009743| ISBN 9781515723738 (library binding) |
ISBN 9781515723776 (pbk.) | ISBN 9781515723813 (ebook (pdf)
Subjects: LCSH: Food--Juvenile literature. | Red—Juvenile literature. |
Color of food—Juvenile literature.
Classification: LCC TX355 .R856 2017 | DDC 641.3—dc23
LC record available at http://lccn.loc.gov/2016009743

Editorial Credits
Megan Atwood, editor; Juliette Peters, designer;
Jo Miller, media researcher; Steve Walker, production specialist

Photo Credits
Images by Capstone Studio: Karon Dubke
Photo styling: Sarah Schuette and Marcy Morin

Printed and bound in China.

PO007712LEOF16

Table of Contents

Red Foods

What does the color
red taste like?
Let's think of red foods.

Red Fruits

Red apples are ripe.

Crunch!

Apples taste tart.

A watermelon grows
on a vine.

The inside is red.

Strawberries smell sweet.

Sniff!

We make jam.

Yum!

Cherries are juicy.

They have pits.

Red Vegetables

Red potatoes have red skin.

Dig them up to eat.

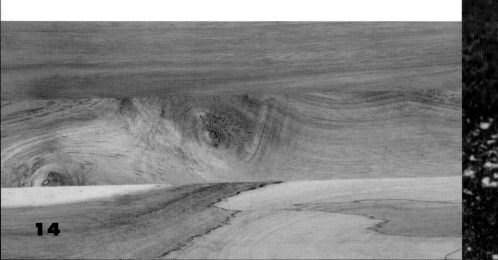

Red peppers grow in a garden.

A red bell pepper is mild.

Red chili peppers are spicy.

bell peppers

chili peppers

Red Meals

My uncle cooks red
beans and rice.
It's my favorite meal!

We eat pasta for lunch.

Tomatoes make the sauce red.

What other foods are red?

Glossary

jam—a sweet, thick spread made with sugar and fruit

mild—a flavor that is gentle in the mouth

pasta—a food made from flour and water

pit—a seed inside some fruits

sauce—a thick liquid eaten with food

spicy—having a strong flavor that feels hot in the mouth

tart—a flavor that tastes a little sour

vine—the stem of fruits or vegetables that grow along the ground

Read More

Glaser, Rebecca Stromstad. *Red.* Colors in Nature. Minneapolis: Bullfrog Books, 2014.

Heos, Bridget. *So You Want to Grow a Pizza?* Grow Your Food. Mankato, Minn.: Amicus, 2016.

Nunn, Daniel. *Red.* Colors All Around Us. Chicago: Heinemann-Raintree, 2012.

Internet Sites

FactHound offers a safe, fun way to find Internet sites related to this book. All of the sites on FactHound have been researched by our staff.

Here's all you do:
Visit *www.facthound.com*
Type in this code: 9781515723738

Super-cool stuff!

Check out projects, games and lots more at
www.capstonekids.com

Index